The Art

Of The

Honey Trap

Dr. Ralph & Catherine Sept

to make a living. In many cases, Honey Traps are brought into to help detectives to fracture hard cases and make dents on the heart of cold-blooded men. In most countries, these beautiful women are called Honey Trap Spies. Many Honey Trap Spies are female agents working deep cover, legally, but the lines become blurred when Honey Trap Spies are employed by illegal covert operations, most time being funded by the government, then the skies are the limit because there is little overhead and "Many Acts" will be permitted to take place. Many illicit acts would include, but not limited to, intercourse, identification theft, extortion, or any other illegal tactic which may be deemed necessary to entrap the "Mark". Most times, when these females are pulled out then the rule book generally goes "Out the Window". Many Honey Traps are more vicious than their male counterparts and act as aggressively. Even though, these women are beautiful are highly dangerous. This is the thing which brings them their allure and spiciness because they are beautiful and deadly. A great majority of Honey Traps usually have a past in the sex industry or a criminal background for minor offenses. In many foreign countries, especially those impoverished, Honey Trap groups are notorious for targeting tourists and unsuspecting natives of that country. Hotbeds of Honey Trap Groups are regions like Asia, India, South America, and countless other destinations. The ranges of these women can be from a highly intelligent woman or someone illiterate, but they understand the power which their femininity brings. In many of the programs, overt and covert, these women operate in clear sight but its usually impossible to detect and this is the mechanism that makes them important to their craft. According to www.atlasobscura.com "These days the "honeypot" is a popular trope in espionage thrillers, with seemingly every high-level informant recruited via seduction by a ravishing female spy. But long before James Bond ever jumped across the roof of a moving train in books or film, the globe-trotting spy Betty Pack was wooing suitors for classified information on both sides of the Atlantic. Few people have elevated the habit of pillow talk to an art form quite like the crafty American-born intelligence officer, who "used the bedroom like <u>Bond used a beretta</u>," *Time* magazine noted in 1963….Pack's code name at the British spy agency MI6 was "Cynthia," and her clandestine escapades during World War II led her boss, Sir William Stephenson, to call her unequivocally "the greatest unsung heroine of the war." Her discovery of the French and Italian naval codes, as well as her work aiding in the decades-long effort to crack the Enigma code, helped the Allies stay a few steps ahead of the Axis powers, and eventually, win the war….In 1936, the election of a pro-communist government in Spain led to the imprisonment of the clergy, including a priest that Betty was intimately acquainted with. After figuring out which prison he had been taken to, she arranged a meeting with the papal nuncio, the diplomatic envoy of the Holy See, and persuaded him to push for the priest's release. Although this was a risky gambit, it worked. Betty then arranged the priest's escape across the border. " It's reasonably to note that many Honey Traps have operated in political capacities such as influencing governmental decisions and manipulating them to make policy changes.

Figure:One Of Greatest M16 Honey Trap Spies, Betty Pack

Many people do not realize that this is the female which was the inspiration for the women in most spy movies and all borrowed little parts of her life. This woman broker deals with the French, Spanish, and South American governments for the release of several high "Marks" including high political targets which had been falsely incarcerated. Later in life, she was called into services to train young Honey Traps the Art of the craft. These powerful women can go places that many others cannot venture and face uncertain death, if discovered, on every mission. While on these missions they enjoy some of the finer things of life, including country clubs, fancy restaurants, and maids and servants at their beckoning call. At a period in her life, she was able to go into any country in the world and she was received as a dignitary. Amazingly, many do not know the craft of Honey Trapping has been around since the beginning of time and they are unable to identify the scheme when it comes to them.

Honey Traps job description mirrors that of trained spies. For us to fully understand the role of a Honey Trap, we must first understand the premise in which they reside. As with a linebacker or quarterback, their positioning does not have much merit unless you understand the arena in which they played. As you delve into their position, you begin to understand the importance of their role and no team could ever achieve victory unless these two important pieces exist on the football team. As with the role of a Honey Trap, women play important roles in their area of specialty and they are generally relied upon to complete an important function: gang stalking and targeting. It would be impossible to fully explain the role of a Honey Trap because their description is highly elusive and changes from target to target. Each Honey Trap is handpicked to play an important part in the life of the targeted individual and without their essential input, many targeted individuals would never fall to their demise. Honey Traps can be mothers, nurses, lawyers, criminals, exotic performers, college students, or any female from all walks of life it all depends upon the assignment. It has been noted that Honey Traps are given acting courses to be proficient in their craft and many used sexuality as a weapon. The same sexuality which enticed the Israelite, Samson to let Delilah shave off his precious locks of hair, in which his strength resided, and delivered him into the hands of the Philistines. These women are trained to use sex as a weapon and in most countries, they are given the green light to engage in sexual intercourse, marriage, and even have kids. Just imagine one of the sexy double spies from the James Bond movies which use manipulation and seduction to reel in the *evening catch* and hand him over into her handlers or the highest bidder. The role of Honey trap is that serious and countless amount of world leaders and men of distinction have fallen to the wrath of the seduction harlots. The role of Honey Traps has been displayed upon many television programs, for example, Good Times when Penny's biological mother wanted her back in her life but could only have her by navigating certain loopholes in the law. This is the basis of the entire targeted program, loopholes and smoke screens. In this case, the role was reversed because there existed the male whore of a Honey Trap called a Honey Dick, Honey Dicks-Man, or Sweet Dick. These men are equally as deadly and deceitful. In this episode, Penny's adoption mother met the gentleman of her dreams which showered her with love, affection, and endless amounts of gifts. The person which Willona thought was the man of her dreams turned out to be a two-bit actor seeking to send Penney back to her abusive Mother. As with Honey Traps and Honey Dicks in real life, the paid perps schemed to have a bogus investigation in which the police would bust the party for drugs, prostitution, and other illegal activity. When the police received a tip they came into to see of the people which the Honey Dick had invited to Willona apartment and when they arrived he denied that he knew anyone. The Honey Traps/Honey Dicks in the real-life targeted program don't just try to set you up, but many have gone as far as poisoning, murdering, and leaving the targeted individual's life into shambles. One targeted individual said, *"Its like she had me in a trance and the more I tried to leave the further she reeled me in until I was permanently "Hooked Like*

Trout" and my life became an everlasting *"Ball of Confusion"*. Moreover, he replied that once he was **"Hooked"** all levels of intimacy disappeared and she did not even want to lay in bed beside him or hug him. Remember, Honey Traps are on assignment and they are to help psychologically break you down and render you ineffective against any forms of covert targeting by the government or private organizations. Another Targeted Individual said, *"That his wife was in on him being involuntarily put in a mental institution while she spent time with her real family in the next city over"*. In this case, they were a married couple for six years and this did not stop her from betraying him for financial gain or undisclosed trinkets. This is the main tactic they employ to get the targeted individual incarcerated or involuntarily put into a mental facility because this destroys the credibility of this person. Once again, to fully grasp the role of a Honey Trap you must begin with the field in which she maneuvers. Most Honey Traps have some level of intelligence because the men who they're targeting or professional business people are those of distinction According to Wikipedia" **Honey Trapping is an investigative practice involving the use of romantic or sexual relationships for interpersonal, political (including state espionage), or monetary purpose.** The Honey Trap makes contact with an individual who has information or resources required by a group or individual which is difficult to obtain without trickery. High level targeted individuals includes Doctors, Lawyers, Professor, Head of Large Corporations, Scientists, Inventors, Chief Civil Right Activists, Authors, Engineers, and those with the potential to empower and make others great. The Honey Trap will then seek to entice the target into a false relationship *(which may or may not include actual physical involvement but Sexual Honey Traps seems to be more effective)*in which they can glean information or influence over the target. Typically, this method is seen to be employed by female operatives against male targets in media depictions, but it has been known to be employed by both genders against a range of targets. For example: when Important foreign guests visit Asian countries a complementary set of females come with their room of choice.

Figure : Asian Honey Trap , Room Service

These women have been trained for years to cipher some bits of information about their guests and report it to their handlers which are most times Asian government officials. According to Wikipedia, **"Private investigators are often employed to create a Honeypot by wives, husbands, and other partners usually when an illicit romantic affair is suspected of the "target", or subject of the investigation. Occasionally, the term may be used for the practice of creating an affair to take incriminating photos for use in blackmail. A Honey Trap is used primarily to collect evidence on the subject of the Honey Trap"**. The natural lure of sexuality makes it nearly impossible for any human being to escape a well designed Honey Trap. For the book, we will explore the Art of Honey Trapping and how it relates to the targeted individual.

Figure: Scotish Honey Trap Enjoying a Box of Expensive Chocolates.

CHAPTER 2

HISTORY OF HONEY TRAPPING

The history of Honey Trapping most likely went back to the beginning of time but consequently, Honey Trapping has been enshrined history in the birthplace of gang stalking, Germany. **According to Foreign Policy Magazine, "The broadest Honey Trap in intelligence history was probably the creation of the notorious East German spymaster, Markus Wolf. In the early 1950s, Wolf recognized that, with marriageable German men killed in large numbers** during World War II and more and more German women turning to careers, the higher echelons of German government, commerce, and industry were now stocked with lonely single women, ripe — in his mind — for the temptations of a Honey Trap. Wolf set up a special department of the Stasi, East Germany's security service, and staffed it with his most handsome, intelligent officers. He called them "Romeo spies." Their assignment was to infiltrate West Germany, seek out powerful, unmarried women, romance them, and squeeze from them all their secrets. Thanks to the Romeo spies and their Honey Traps, the Stasi penetrated most levels of the West German government and industry. At one stage, the East Germans even had a spy inside NATO who was able to give information on the West's deployment of nuclear weapons. Another used her connections to become a secretary in the office of the West German chancellor, Helmut Schmidt. The scheme lost its usefulness when the West German counterintelligence authorities devised a simple way of identifying the Stasi officers as soon as they arrived in West Germany: They sported distinctly different haircuts — the practical "short back and sides" variety instead of the fashionable, elaborate West German style. Alerted by train guards, counterintelligence officers would follow the Romeo spies and arrest them at their first wrong move. Three of the women were caught and tried, but in general, the punishment was lenient. One woman who managed to penetrate West German intelligence was sentenced to only six and a half years in prison, probably because ordinary West Germans had some sympathy with the women. Wolf himself faced trial twice after the collapse of communism but received only a two-year suspended sentence, given the confusion of whether an East German citizen could be guilty of treachery to West Germany." Therefore, the art of Honey Trapping ranges back for many years. The craft was especially useful with the mob and gangs of the 1950-70s. **"Marks"** would be baited by a beautiful seductress and would later be kidnapped and many people were killed in the process.

Figure : German Honey Trap On A Picnic In Large Field of Daisies

West Germany identified the usefulness of the craft and used it against many of their enemies including political opponents. It is recognized by many nations that the lure of sex is too difficult to resist. In the days of the mob, Honey Traps were used to help broker sweet deals with the enemy and find out important information about drug shipments and crimes committed. Honey Traps have influenced the decisions of Judges and men of great power and honor. One of the greatest mysteries is the story of recording artist, Sam Cooke and his demise in a seedy motel in Compton, California in 1964. According to Performingsongwriter.com"

When their orders arrived, Al Schmitt went to get Sam and found him laughing it up with a group of friends and music business associates. Sam was buying, and he flashed a wad of bills, what looked like thousands of dollars. He told Al that he and his wife should go ahead with their meal. At a booth near the bar, there was a baby-faced 22-year-old Asian girl, sitting with three guys. Sam caught her eye. He'd seen her around. One of the guys, a guitar player Sam knew, introduced them. The girl's name was Elisa Boyer. Before long, the pair were cozied up in a booth...Was Sam Cooke lured into a trap at the Hacienda Motel? Were Elisa Boyer and Bertha Franklin working in tandem? Was Barbara Cooke involved somehow? Or was it all just a tragic accident? Over the years, various investigators have made noises about reopening the case, but with most of the principle players dead and gone, it seems unlikely it will ever be solved. ."

Figure 1: This Woman Resemble the Woman From the Sam Cooke Story,

Sam Cooke was widely admired, by fans of all

colors, he was ahead of his time, and a cultural icon. He began to associate with controversial figures like Muhammad Ali, Malcolm X, Jim Brown, and others. In FBI documents, Sam Cooke was identified as a popular negro singer from California. According to a member of one of his groups, " Sam was not a Muslim, he was only interested in the economical part of what the Muslims wanted to do for the black community, not religion. This would be a balance statement because he abandoned religion for a secular music career and sought to open his recording and booking agency catering strictly to negro artists. Sam was lured by a beautiful Asian Honey Trap in a bar one evening after he came off the road with about five thousand dollars in his pocket. The story is unclear but at the end of the night, Mr. Sam Cooke was murdered in the seedy hotel room he shared with this Asian Honey Trap which destroyed his legacy forever. One of his recording artists revealed," Man, Sam use to get all kinds of people coming to the office saying, "Sam,

WE believe you should forget about owning your own record company. According to the documentary these were members of the mob who highly controlled the music industry. These activities were also relevant to shady individuals in Germany. According to Wikipedia, "Salon Kitty was a high-class Berlin **brothel** used by the Nazi intelligence service, the **Sicherheitsdienst** (SD), for **espionage** purposes during **World War II**. Created in the early 1930s, the salon was taken over by SS general **Reinhard Heydrich** and his subordinate **Walter Schellenberg** in 1939. The brothel was managed by original owner Kitty Schmidt throughout its entire existence. The plan was to seduce top German dignitaries and foreign visitors, as well as diplomats, with alcohol and women so they would disclose secrets or express their honest opinions on Nazi-related topics and individuals...he idea to use Salon Kitty for espionage purposes was **Reinhard Heydrich**'s, a leading SS general and police chief within **Nazi Germany**. Instead of infiltrating the brothel, Schellenberg took it over altogether. The idea was to entertain prominent guests with wine and women, so they would disclose secrets or talk about their real opinions to ensure their support could be relied upon. The nine rooms of the salon were lavishly expanded and renovated to the highest standards of the 1930s. Schellenberg installed **covert listening devices** in the rooms and converted the basement into a "workshop" where five operators could make transcriptions of conversations from the love-making rooms. For the purpose of espionage, the SS started looking for young women to work in the brothel. In a circular deemed "top secret", Schellenberg asked administrative offices in Berlin for assistance. The requirement profile read: "Wanted are women and girls, who are intelligent, multilingual, nationalistically minded and furthermore man-crazy" (Gesucht werden arrested dozens of Berlin prostitutes and selected the most attractive as potential agents to work at Salon Kitty. Among other things, they were trained to recognize military uniforms, and to glean secrets from innocuous conversation. They were not told about the microphones, but had to make a report after every encounter. The ladies all had their particular attractions and had been trained to satisfy even the discerning customers. Historian **Paul Roland** further notes that the women who entertained members of the Nazi elite, however, were respected ladies of Berlin's high society who were given no allowances for their "contributions" and were nearly all married to men of good financial means." This is a clear example of the women chosen for these highly important operations which netted many of the most elite in German's circle because their guards were let down after sexual satisfaction. As with many Honey Traps on today, rarely are they told the gist of the operation because the fear of human error and the disclosure of the investigation for covert operation. As with the targeted program, many of these Honey Traps were employed by J.

Edgar Hoover and the Federal Bureau of Investigations to perform investigation when they crushed the mafia activity such organized crime, illegal alcohol distribution, and other illicit activities. The opposition utilizing whatever weakness is exhibited by the "Mark or Target". The sexual orientation of individuals in the past have always been a delicate subject because of the moral values of most people in society at that time. Homosexuality was frowned upon in all segments of the world especially those individuals who are in public service. **According to Foreign Policy Magazine,** "Not all Honey Traps are heterosexual ones. In fact, during less tolerant eras, a homosexual Honey Trap with a goal of blackmail could be just as effective as using women as bait. Take the tragic story of Jeremy Wolfenden, the London Daily Telegraph's correspondent in Moscow in the early 1960s. Wolfenden was doubly vulnerable to KGB infiltration: He spoke Russian, and he was gay. Seizing its opportunity, the KGB ordered the Ministry of Foreign Trade's barber to seduce him and put a man with a camera in Wolfenden's closet to take compromising photos.The KGB then blackmailed Wolfenden, threatening to pass on the photographs to his employer if he did not spy on the Western community in Moscow. Wolfenden reported the incident to his embassy, but the official British reaction was not what he expected. On his next visit to London, he was called to see an officer from the Secret Intelligence Service (SIS) who asked him to work as a double agent, leading the KGB along but continuing to report back to SIS. The stress led Wolfenden into alcoholism. He tried to end his career as a spy, marrying a British woman he had met in Moscow, arranging a transfer from Moscow to the Daily Telegraph's Washington bureau, and telling friends he had put his espionage days behind him. But the spy life was not so easily left behind. After encountering his old SIS handler at a British Embassy party in Washington in 1965, Wolfenden was again pulled back into the association. His life fell into a blur of drunkenness. On Dec. 28, 1965, when he was 31, he died, apparently from a cerebral hemorrhage caused by a fall in the bathroom. His friends believed, no matter what the actual cause of death, that between them, the KGB and the SIS had sapped his will to live. Ironically, his time as a spy probably produced little useful material for either side. His colleagues weren't giving him any information because they were warned that he was talking to the KGB, and the Soviets weren't likely to give him anything either. In this case, the Honeypot proved deadly — with little purpose for anyone." In this case, His weaknesses were catalog and used his homosexual background as a weapon against him. The gist of a Honey Traps' effectiveness is metered by the responses and outcomes experienced by the victim. Most Honey Traps are as deadly as a black widow spider seeking to get close enough to strike her next victim.

Figure : Male Version of A Honey Trap

CHAPTER 3

WHAT IS THE TARGETED PROGRAM

Targeted individual program, in the United States, extends back to the Patriot Act enacted by George W. Bush, but there is evidence that the program extended back before World War 2 and linked directly to Adolf Hitler. The American people approve of this countermeasure gave the government/law enforcement more power in the wake of the 9/11 attacks on the Twin Towers/World Trade Centers in New York. The only problem is that countless amount of innocent people were wrongly placed on a terrorist watch list for the wrong reasons, mostly hard working American citizens. The watch list soon included members of society like activists, authors, lawyers, and anyone which the federal government deemed a threat?! There was one case of a Ninety Nine year old man being targeted by this ridiculous harassment program. The techniques were brokered out to private security companies like InfraGard which carries out much of the targeting of individuals on the watch list. The Patriot Act gave powerful entities of the government the green light to invade upon the rights of millions of Americans, but interestingly, the contents of the targeted program have been initiated on every continent of the world, not limited to just the largest countries. The target program employs, in the words of George W. Bush, *"unsavory characters"*, to bring about the wickedness of this murderous program. The information shows that individuals who are placed upon this list are seldom removed meaning this a death program. Jews or sympathetic Germany which were placed in the concentration camps where they were there for life; just like the target program utilized, today. The program is a race, gender, socioeconomically-based neutral program which utilized the aspects of psychology, physiology, science, chemistry, and even parts of black magic to propel this death program on the unlucky individuals who have been selected for this program. There is no notice to inform you that you have fallen on this illegal Terrorist Watch list which is composed of people who are grandmothers, children, women, men, intellects, and highly educated individuals who have never committed a crime in their entire lives. They are highly aware that these are good citizens so many great efforts are made to make these people into criminals with false files, bogus investigations, misleading information, unsubstantiated rumors, lies, and other slanderous components to destroy the lives of those which have become a part of this death fraternity. Even those which are responsible to bring us the news are in cahoots with keeping the bases of this program hidden from plain sight, but with the invention of the internet it allowed citizens to compare notes of things which have been happening in their lives to come to the conclusion that all these events are systematic and occurring with many people around the world. The targeted program is created to keep the targeted individual unbalanced and in a state of confusion in which vital information is collected twenty-four hours a day. Along with the Targeted/ Zersetzung Stasi Program, there is also the initiation of human experimentation, violation of civil and human rights, and defamation of character campaigns. For example, the Tuskegee experiment utilized illegal covert studies against African American men. According to Wikipedia, " *Tuskegee Study of Untreated Syphilis in the Negro Male was a clinical study conducted between 1932 and 1972 by the U.S. Public Health Service. The purpose of this study was to observe the natural history of untreated syphilis; the African-American men in the study were only told they were receiving free health care from the United States government. Programs such as MK Ultra, Operation Cointelpro, and other programs are forerunners to the Targeted Program which has been in enacted in the 21st Century.* These program has been utilized to suppress many facets of society not limited to activists, journalists, free thinkers, and many individuals which may have taken a stand against corruption on the part of the government, powerful financial entities, or private citizens which have connections to powerful sources. The basis of this program is controlled through illegal vices, lies, manipulation, theft, discrediting, bullying, fear, and any means to destroy those which fall outside their grid of acceptable thinking(Hive Mind). As you will see farther in this book that the components of this program have a highly spiritually influenced from bribing, seeking to identify mental and physical weaknesses or anything which will render the Targeted Citizen helpless at the mercy of the Deep State. The goal of the program is to keep society in a sorta ignorant utopia of the many ills which are transpiring beneath their very noses. The program is so wicked and cunning that it employs the evilness used by Satan himself for financial, political, and strategic gain. For the individual which have the intelligence to *"peep beyond the veil"* of corruption there are great attempts to keep these individuals silent, even though, all they need to do is simply ask the person not to divulge the information which has been uncovered instead of going as far as putting them on a watch list for life. The fear that the public would find out propels these groups to wrath with military persistence. First, there are many layers of the targeted program because several Targeted Individuals have confessed the many levels in which they have been tortured. This program is enacted by several different entities, including the government, which have invested heavily in the success of the Targeted Program. Most would agree that this is the money, torture, and death program because many people are enlisted to perform tasks, acts, and duties which they would not perform under the usual circumstances. For example, a retired elementary school teacher engaging in mercenary activities to supplement her income. Some might say it is the **"Temptation program"** or the **"too good to be true program"** because perpetrators are being paid to do virtually nothing for large amounts of cash, gifts, and other prizes.

Many are thrilled because they feel a sense of importance because they are providing services to a law enforcement body; generally, patriotic. Consequently, the program is far from patriotic but murderous in nature and based on lies, deceits, and an abundance of half-truths. Most **"perps or gang-stalkers"** are generally *kept in the dark* about the true intent of the duties in which they are performing. At some point, all perps or gang stalkers become aware that the line of work they are participating in is highly illegal but the money is so good that they cannot resist the financial gain involved in this program. These perps even operate in churches, hospitals, funerals, and anywhere they are instructed to venture and are *head over heels* about making that easy money. Some perps are pastors, deacons, doctors, lawyers, judges, and other powerful people of distinction. Even those which have had a change of heart must continue with the program because resistance would surely land their names to be added to one of the terrorist watch lists to be tortured. The programs seek confusion among citizens and amplify the effects to the point where there is total disruption. The Targeting program identifies strength and mainly look for shortcomings to attack the intended target in a *no holds barred* type elimination fashion.

CHAPTER 4

THE EFFECTS OF TARGETED PROGRAM ON SOCIETY

There exist a great gulf of knowledge between the Targeted Individual and the general public as a whole. Many Targeted Individuals are mislabeled and slanderous rumors are cast about the discredit those which the government dislikes. Due to the covert nature of the Targeted program, most Americans have been kept in the dark about a large number of taxpayers' dollars being wasted upon this touchless torture platform. This is the torture program because the goal is to drive you to lunacy, suicide, or commit some criminal infraction to get you locked up for a long period of time. The program is a depopulation scheme designed to deceive the most intelligent individuals of the basis and intent and many are duped into participation without even giving a second thought. The uniqueness of the program bypasses race, religion, gender, and socioeconomic status to implode the structures of society from the *inside-out*. The mixture of this program supersedes the imagination

41

of the most skilled novelists, authors, or writers because the plot could not be dreamed up in your wildest imagination. The covertness of the program makes it foolproof that it is being exposed to the average citizen would be nearly impossible to detect. There are more people who are willing to say that life exists upon Mars than to admit a program as prevalent as the Targeted program exists under their very noses. That is the beauty of this program, in a sick, twisted, and demonic way, it operates clearly in plain view but is invisible to society as a whole, and; even those which are provided proof will still deny that a program of this magnitude could be operating in also-called free society. A society with agreed-upon modes of behavior, laws, and morally-based where each citizen is guaranteed his day in court. Even in ancient Egypt, under the Les Talons platform, they got their day in court. With this program, there is no formal announcement that you are on the Targeted Program and it is your duty to find out on your own that the life in which you have built since birth would never exist the way it had been prior. Absolutely, no inclination that personal relationships built over a lifetime would be destroyed over the matter of a few months. There are countless relationships, marriages, families, friendships, and acquaintances which are lost due to this hideous program. The effects of this program are that it disrupts the function of countless citizens and severs the relationships of even more human beings. The Targeted Program cost society trillions of dollars because many innocent citizens are incarcerated, institutionalized, or not permitted to provide to the financial structure of the world. This program compromises the integrity of the government which we have been taught to abide, believe, and rely upon for guidance. For example: Until President Donald J. Trump revealed that there was a **"Deep State"** or **"Fake News"** and most citizens would not have believed that most programming is generally compromised and if it's on the news it must be the truth. When these types of revelations are revealed it makes citizens question other things which they may have been misled to falsely believe.

CHAPTER 5

ASPECTS OF THE ILLEGAL GANG STALKING

PROGRAM

First of all, the illegal stalking program can be traced to Adolf Hitler and the German nation. The tactics of gang-stalking were utilized against the Jews and German Citizens which refused to cooperate. Adolf Hitler's Zersetzung Stasi Program is the exact same program being used on Targeted Individuals, today. According to Dr. Eric Karlstrom,

"**The Stasi, as follows:**

1. Spied on the population, mainly through a vast network of citizens turned informants (watchdogs)

2. Used overt and covert methods of attack

3. Used psychological warfare/psychological

destruction of their dissidents

4. Espionage

5. Surveillance of mail and telephone

   communications

6. Analyzed garbage

7. Sabotaged

8. Used armed forces

9. Operated in all foreign countries

10. Surveillance of foreigners

11. Coordinated its work with Soviet

   Intelligence Agencies

12. The Stasi trained and/or helped

   build secret police for others

   including Ethiopia, Cuba,

   Egypt, People's Republic of

   Angola, the People's Republic of

   Mozambique, and the

People's Republic of

Yemen (South Yemen), Syria, etc.

13.Operated its own penal system which comprised of prison camps for political, as opposed to, criminal offenders

14.Less mentally and academically-endowed candidates were made ordinary soldiers/agents

15.Infiltration of the residential areas, schools, universities, and hospitals of their victims. Reporting of victim visitations, including all family and friends.

16.Privacy Invasion-Drilled holes in apartments and hotel rooms and filmed citizens with special video cameras

17.Formal categorizations of victims

18.Informants were made to feel important, given material or social incentives, and were imbued with a sense of adventure, and only around 7.7%, according to official figures, were coerced into cooperating. They frequently employed the use of blackmail. In some cases, spouses spied on one another.

19.Gas lighting/Psychological

Harassment/Zersetzung
*Zersetzung generally involved the disruption of the victim's private or family life. This often included psychological attacks such as breaking into homes and messing with the contents – moving furniture, altering the timing of an alarm, removing pictures from walls or replacing one variety of tea with another. Other practices included property damage, sabotage of cars, purposely incorrect medical treatment, smear campaigns including sending falsified compromising photos or documents to the victim's family, denunciation, provocation, psychological warfare, psychological subversion, wiretapping, bugging, mysterious phone calls or unnecessary deliveries, even including sending a vibrator to a target's wife.

20.Arrest and Torture

21.Disinformation

22.They operated brothels. Also, agents were used against both men and women working in Western governments. "Entrapment" was used against married men and homosexuals.

23.Sent sleeper agents to other countries

(namely the West)

24.The Stasi channeled large amounts of money to Neo-Nazi groups in West, with the purpose of discrediting the West.

25.Used armed weapons

26.Assassinated using death squads, kidnapped, poisoned victims, etc.

27.Assisted in the cover-up of traces to a crime

It seems that the Stasi and the programs of Gang Stalking have much in common. It was amazing to find that the Stasi's agenda from past history has been mirrored in the lives of today's Targeted Individuals who suffer the terroristic threat of gang stalking. Is it really a coincidence that they both seem as if they are one and the same?" The general scope of gang stalking is harassment to the highest level of destructive practices designed to interrupt the lives of those citizens illegally placed in these programs. Gang-stalking is an organized practice by members of society to reach a certain defined goal to cleansing the community of people who are less desirable. The program's design is strategically placed to make the target feel his/her life is worthless. The programs make you question your abilities, weaknesses, and even your belief in God. The program is based to make you question, Why would God allow me to go through such evil things? What did I do to deserve this type of torture? I know many others who have done far worse things than myself. The program causes many questions to arise about the purpose of having such a wicked-based program. Most elements of the Targeted Program are parallel to the elements woven deeply within the confines of spiritual warfare and biblical aspects because most historians would agree that the Targeted Program has a Lucifer undertone and navigates deeply to that demonic possession and human control mechanisms. As with the Honey Trap, she slithers her way into the lives of unsuspecting men and causes mountains of confusion.

CHAPTER 6

MS. HONEY TRAPPER

The Honey Trap acts as a **"lure, tackle, and bait"** to entice the targeted individual as a centerpiece to fulfill all his wildest dreams. The studying phase of the targeted program becomes particularly important because the handlers which hand-craft the Honey Trap to be exactly what the targeted

individual desires.

For example, I am particularly attracted to strong-minded independent women and this is the kind of Honey Trap they tried to send at me and utilized a family member to set up the meeting. According to my family member, "She is a smart, attractive, religious woman, which reads the Bible and pray exactly the way you do". Despite being married, these handlers have absolutely no consideration for your wife and family. I must admit if I was not aware of this program and had not been married then meeting this woman would have been a *no-brainer*. Once again, your likes and dislikes are cataloged and used for future projects. For example, The Handlers are aware that you are particularly fond of a usual favor of ice cream or you like your cappuccino prepared in a certain way. The Handlers would create a skit where the Honey Trap would be at the same creamery you frequent and she will sit directly beside you and would loudly order, the exact same ice cream or beverage which you have ordered since you were a kid and this is the point in which the conversation erupts between you and the

Targeted Individual. Oddly, you and this woman have so many things in common from watching the same movies, admiring the exact leaders, and you walk her to her vehicle to exchange numbers and she has a rare CD which is your favorite artist in the world. This appears to be a match in Heaven but soon it would become one from Hell. It was reported by one YouTuber that he married a Honey Trap and had many kids and grandkids. It was only years later that he determined that this woman was spying on him for financial gains. As he reminisced and reviewed in 20/20 hindsight he began to fill in mysterious behavior, missing money, and unaccounted for time. Not only was this woman a farce but she was a straight-up fraud. This lady had been on long term assignment designed to make this man's life a living Hell. Honey Trap relationships have several things in common: they begin with a steamy romance and a *foot on the after-effects of the break* which include arguments, gaslighting, and countless disagreements. The relationship is similar to a drug that quickly enters the system and causes you to **"crash"** without notice. You find yourself constantly struggling to get back to the place in which the relationship was so steamy, dreamy, and full of passion. In short, most Honey Traps are told to hit the cool down phase right before marriage or constantly string the target on that this event would take place in the near future. The make of the Honey Trap is designed to fulfill the article of the organized community stalking program by leaving the **"Mark"** let down and in a state of confusion.

Principles   Honey Trap Achieves *1. You are unable to create stable relationships with the closest people in your life 2. Propel the notion that no one is stalking you its all in your mind, 3. Keep you from joyful intimacy which comes with being in a fruitful relationship. The Honey Trap relationship is like having an older vehicle in which you must constantly spend funds for repairs. The more you repair the more it needs more updates.   4. The Honey Trap sabotage friendships, financial opportunities, and* *gainful outlooks upon the future. Honey Traps are trained to never let you leave the relationship.* For example, you may say,"I **am leaving this relationship"** and she immediately asks **"Why you must go"**.The scheme is blown when the Targeted Individual is permitted to exit the relationship which means that she will no longer be getting paid for her illicit services. By keeping you in this dammed relationship she is fully compensated because it is meeting the terms of her gang stalking job description. Her job indeed is a pick you up and let you down on so many levels. Many targeted individuals remain in these relationships because they are reluctant to meet new people because of their status as a targeted individual or an individual illegally placed upon a governmental watch list. Even after they suspect their affectionate other is a Honey Trap they still remain in the relationship. Many Honey Traps are used against individuals unfortunate to be placed on a covert government watch list. According to Wikipedia, *"Each* *assignment varies depending on what the agent and client decide on during their prior consultation. A common assignment consists of the agent initiating contact with the subject through <u>face-to-face interaction</u>. The agent will attempt to take the communication further into other outlets including: e-mail, text messaging, phone calls, etc. The step after this can be considered the most crucial moment of the assignment. The agent will propose a second meeting to the subject. Whether or not the subject agrees to further communication will determine whether the assignment will go deeper or come to an end. <u>Hotels</u> are often used as a meeting place...but to determine whether the subject intends for the relationship to escalate. Once the investigation comes to an end, the agent will turn over any record of communication they had with the subject. Other documents that are recorded include: photographs, videos, venue appointments, etc".*

Reasons that Targeted Individual Remain in a Relationship with a Honey Trap.

1. Sex

2. Companionship

3. Denial

4. Finances

5. Children

6. Property Attained

7. Hope they to Change Them

8. Feeling and hopelessness, despair, and loneliness they would never be able to find another mate.

1. Sex/Intimacy

In the same way that all humans need food, water, and shelter, most would agree, that sex and intimacy must also go down as one of those important essential desires wanted by every human being. Even the animals created by God have an urgency to reproduce through the act of intimacy. Targeted Individual's threshold is much higher because most have been through broken relationships and have had sexual droughts, over years and months, unless you include masturbation. Therefore, many Targeted Individuals will stay with a woman because she can please his needs. A beautiful Honey Trap will almost certainly be difficult to replace especially if the Targeted Individual may not be handsome or a good catch for most women. This is another reason sexy women are chosen for the program because it's nearly impossible for men to give these beautiful women up. The attraction of sexual satisfaction always pulls targeted individuals back in the same Honey Trap position. He will do the simplest things just to have someone for sexual satisfaction, especially a beautiful woman. Even in the cool-down phase, the Honey Trap stops being intimate with the Targeted Individual and he continues to hang around for a chance to be intimate even if it happens once a year. Gangstalking friends and family also helps to keep the Honey Trap in the Targeted Individual's life by reminding him,**"Man, where is your fine old** lady? Man, don't let that fox get away from you, a lot of men would be happy to hook up with her." Even though, she is beautiful, in reality, she is a train wreck waiting to derail your life. It has been reported that the Honey Trap will intentionally have sex with friends, family, enemies, or anything to hurt the Targeted Individual. Honey Traps are given large bonuses each time they break the Targeted Individual's heart. Their job is to carry out the plan of the Gangstalking organizers which sent them and falling in love is against the policy and highly forbidden for the Honey Trap. For Honey Traps which have unfortunately acquired feelings for the Targeted Individual, they will be replaced or become a target, also. This means each time she goes to work with the targeted individual it is a big deal and confidentiality is pivotal. According to Targeted Individuals, governmental groups like the Department of Justice, FBI, NSA, DOD cipher valuable information using Honey Traps which would otherwise be impossible to attain

Figure: Honey Traps Are Women of Many Secrets.

without this valuable tool. Through sexual satisfaction, human beings have a tendency to let their guards down and open up to the person in which they are engaging. During this relaxed mode, immediately following sex, the Targeted Individual may be so happy and relaxed that he may reveal something which is highly valuable in an investigation or import secret which may be cataloged and used at a later date. This information may be used to entrap, set up, and harass the targeted individual. The Honey Trap moves as stealth as a season FBI agent collecting hard to get information that could not be achieved by no other individual. During sexual intimacy, they are encouraged to be high adventurous, fulfill all requests, and perform to the highest level to capture the trust of the Targeted Individual. The governmental agency discovers that the targeted individual has always desired to be with more that one female to wiretap conversation then the Honey Trap will insist that they become more exploratory and include others in their sexual playtime. Many women employed as Honey Traps are former people who worked in the sex industry, such as strippers and prostitutes, and they are comfortable performing at an exceptional sexual level. Once again this is one of the greatest factors which prevent targeted individuals from leaving and he realizes that he is depended upon the Honey Trap and this is the "Hook and Trap" part of the engagement. The sexual attraction almost becomes hypnotic as the targeted individual becomes heavy depended upon someone who is undependable/unreliable. The level of misguidance is the thing that causes many targeted individuals to commit suicide which is also one of the factors and goals of the organized community harassment program. The meaning of the program is to keep you in a state of disarray and unbalanced until many mistakes many be made on your behalf.

The Reason That Sexual Factors Are So Important in the Honey Trap Scheme

A. Sex is a human factor that allows the Targeted Individual to put his guards down and leaves him unprotected.

B. Sex is used as a "Bait and Hook" ploy to

provide an illustration of a fruit relationship which will have

an unpleasant outcome.

C. During the turmoil stage of the Honey Trap scheme, the Targeted Individual may become so distraught that they may engage in alcohol/drug abuse which will lead to life long addiction farther breaking down the good character of the Targeted Individual and meeting the goals of the program.

D. Once the Honey Trap has full access to the emotions of the Targeted Individual he becomes ripen for manipulation such as criminal behaviors.

E. On occasions, Honey Traps have to used in criminal warfare tactics by knowingly giving the Targeted Individual an incurable disease to lead to certain death or despair.

2. Companionship

As mentioned prior, most Targeted Individuals crave the opposition sexual interaction because all legitimate relationships have been destroyed by those heading the Organized community gang stalking. They would actually create rumors and lies to bring forth their destructive objectives. The program is designed that the Targeted Individual must be isolated this is the reason they destroy or compromise all relationships with family, friends, and the opposite sex. This is also completed to make way for the placement of their Honey Traps, agents, and operatives to be put closest to the Targeted Individual at all times. Many dedicated family members/friends risked being targeted if they provide assistance to the Targeted Individual. Many Targeted Individuals have complained about family and friend mysterious passing away. Once these key people are compromised or replaced it allows the illegal covert program a better opportunity to penetrate the Targeted Individual. The hungry for human interaction makes the Targeted Individual susceptible to making wrong choices and becoming entwined with the wrong individuals. There are countless people in prison and institutions reflecting back upon how the closest people in their lives along with the government to set them up. The drive of loneliness is especially difficult for men or women who may have recently lost a companion or a loved one to this evil program. The handler seizes this as a grand opportunity to put the right people in place to carry forth their roost and eliminate the targeted individual. Companionship is one of the most important factors in human psyche because it provides acceptance and wanting attention from the opposite sex to fill the void of losing a loved one. *According to psychology today,"**There are a lot of ways that psychologist and researchers try to quantify the health of a relationship. Some look at the quantity of positive interactions, others ask about satisfaction, and another group looks at how needs get met by partners. The latter is centrally important in working therapeutically with couples, and I hope the following post will highlight some*** information that readers can apply to their own relationships or groups of friends. The basic relationship needs written about here are all things that we cannot provide ourselves, and we rely on others to help provide them for us. The original concept about this kind of need was from psychoanalytic therapists who called them "dependency needs", because we were dependent on others to meet them. Specifically, when we are first born into the world, almost every need except for oxygen is a dependency need. An infant is dependent on caregivers for food, comfort, care, etc. As we get older, these needs change because we learn to provide some of these things for ourselves. However, as adults, there is still a universal set of relationship needs that remain. These are For couples, these needs are ideally met in the partnership. Strong couples are able to be good companions (sharing their day to day lives, personal histories, and interests together), give verbal and physical affection (affirmations, hugs, sexual *intimacy, compliments, etc), and provide emotional support (being there to help during tough times, validations when the person is struggling, etc). In a healthy relationship, both members of a couple get used to depending on the other for these needs, and when they are not met, each person starts to become dissatisfied, which ultimately can lead to a break up. For a good model on fulfilling these in your relationship, read "Healthy Relationships".Individuals that are not currently in a partnership need to have these met in other ways. Usually a lot of this occurs in strong bonds with friends and family. A good example would be a group of friends or a family that knows you well, gives big hugs when they see you, always get your back and know the right thing to say when you are under stress, and make you feel like you have an important place in their lives."*The Illegally organized understand this principle best and they are wicked enough to use it as a weapon. As with the targeted program, the governmental watch listing seeks to mimic the confinements of prison but one that is virtual without bars and they propel this by their illegally destroying all friendships and contacts. The Honey is greatly used to create distance between family and friend and keep up on array of confusion to leave the targeted individual under her control. *According to Psychology Today, "The results of these needs not being met are different depending on the individual on where he or she is in life. If these needs are not met when we are children, it can lead to longer lasting problems relating to others. As adults, not having these met adequately leads to feelings of loneliness and sometimes can move into hopelessness or depression. Most adults can manage some periods of time without these being adequately met, but it is important for our overall health that they are attended to. Unfortunately, many family cultures and role expectations in the United States dismiss the importance of these needs, and instill values that not needing these things is somehow a superior way of being. When a person holds these values, and these needs are not met, there can be a compounded level of shame and distress, which is more complicated to work through. These can also get in the way of meeting the needs of your partner or friends. Some examples of values or beliefs that interfere with these are: "I don't need anyone", "I can always rely on myself", "I don't want to burden others with my problems", "crying or being angry doesn't solve anything", and "I only say 'i love you' infrequently because it will mean more when I say it".* "Even babies have an innate need to be picked up, nurtured, or cradled and many will cry when they are not shown attention. Adults cry out in a different way and many times they seek to self medicate with drugs and alcohol to fill certain voids in their lives. This is useful to the Honey Trap because she moves in and becomes his reason to live by filling all nooks and crannies. The loss of a companion has made many targeted individuals give up because they no longer see a reason for living and this is the feeling that the

Honey Traps seek to display to the targeted individual.

3. Denial

A large majority of Target individuals struggle with denying their significant other is a Honey Trap. Generally, there must exist mountains of evidence for the Targeted Individual to phantom that the love of his life is a Honey Trap. In the majority of cases, the targeted individual becomes so brainwashed he is **"Silly Putty"** in the Honey Traps' palms. As with family members and others who are unable to see the Organized community program operational state, so is the targeted individual engaged with a Honey Trap. He is totally blinded about the intentions of this woman he loves with all his heart. The rules of most Honey Trap relationships are that she controls the "flow and rhythm" of the program. Many times, Honey Traps engage high level targeted individuals and are paid by powerful entities and go as far as bearing children for the targeted individual, but these types of clearances must be assigned from the higher levels of the targeted individual program. Remember that these programs are financially based which means that many Honey Traps would be more than willing to have a child for the targeted individual because the child can be used for greater leverage against the targeted individual. Especially targeted individuals who have greater levels of finances or may be wealthy. The Honey Trap will seek to take a great portion or all the assets of the targeted individual, and in many cases, corrupt Judges in on the organized community harassment program will ensure that would be the final result. The important thing to understand is it would be more difficult for the targeted individual to exit the relationship/marriage if children are involved because to deny the Honey Trap is to deny his blood offspring. Furthermore, the scheme gets more interesting for passive targeted individuals because many times they will have children for their real lover and put the children on the targeted individual which equals an eighteen-year contract. The children may be used as a weapon on greater levels especially whenever arguments occur because she will allude **"These are not your children anyhow"** to further breakdown the targeted individual. In most cases, the Honey Trap despises the targeted individual which makes her job easier to perform wicked things to this innocent individual. Nearly all targeted individuals are innocent because they never had their day in court. The only defense against an aggressive Honey Trap is to identify the scheme early so you have an opportunity to exit the relationship. The more your life and the Honey Trap become intertwined, the more difficult it is to leave the relationship. The scheme is designed that the savviest targeted individuals will not have the power to exit the relationship because this person is specially created to satisfy your deepest desires. The loneliness and isolation of many targeted individuals also work in favor of the Honey Trap because some company is better than no company at all. To add insult to injury, many of the children bore in these illicit relationships fully have an outside relationship with their biological father. In some cases, the biological father may be introduced as an uncle, cousin, or long lost relative seeking to intermingle with your children. *Tell-tell signs* that the children may be his is apparent if this person purchases many elaborate gifts and gives attention that only a father could provide. This person would be around for birthdays, special holidays, and emergencies that are experienced by the children. The denial tugs at the targeted individual many times but he is reluctant or unable to break free of the Honey Trap arrangement. The targeted individual has become a prisoner of this relationship.

4. Finances

Some Honey Traps will come along with many "Bells and Whistles" such as providing finances to cash strapped targeted individuals. These Honey Traps are given high clearances, budgets, and luxuries to spend on the targeted individual. Most times, the wining and dining period is extremely short just to get the targeted individual to comply with the demands of the Honey entrapment. Whenever a targeted individual is concerned, rest assured, there will never be an extended period of luxuries because the scope of the program is to leave him broke, homeless, and alone. These Honey Traps will approach the targeted individual bearing gifts or a good financial opportunity. For example: "I am a prostitute and I need you to be my pimp or boss". If the targeted individual falls for this scheme he may wind up in federal prison according to the circumstances surrounding their engagement. Also, with finances, the Honey Trap may provide care to a targeted individual which may have fallen ill to gain his trust. This will be something she will always remind the targeted individual whenever he seeks to exit the relationship. There may also be certain connections that the Honey Trap can get for the targeted individual which he may not be able to do on his own. If the targeted individual has a small business she may introduce him to clients. Generally, these connections are setups and stings to illegally entrapment the targeted individual. These people will appear genuine on the outside but would be working directly with the police. In the State of Louisiana, there was a sting that entrapped many black mayors of small cities. It is believed that these men were taken to strip clubs where some may have been introduced to women of the night. This is considered targeting on a larger scale because the stripper in the facility may be told," We need one of y'all to get him laid". Even though those who are directly involved in the sting cannot have sex with the targeted person, this does not apply to Honey Traps particular in a large strip club typesetting. As with companionship, finances are very essential to life and it is impossible to be relevant in the world without them. This is the reason the targeting program aims to keep the targeted individual "broke".The Honey Trap reassures the targeted individual that, "We are in this together because we are a team". In short, all we got is us and propels this belief to him, daily. There have been targeted individuals who have known that the Honey Trap was a perp, but still played the game and eventually fell in love because she is so convincing. In many respects, the Honey Trap is a psychiatrist of sorts because she is able to complete many feats with the mind of the targeted individual and he may become her "Sugar Daddy or Financier".

Figure: Beautiful & Cunning Honey Trap

5. Children

As aforementioned above, children can play a key role in the targeting of a gang stalking victim. The children do not necessarily have to be for the target individual, but he will eventually adopt them as his own. It is very difficult for a person which has been in total isolation, find a makeshift family, and give them up, without recourse. The creators of the program are aware of this "needing" behavior and they use it to their full advantage. One targeted individual commented, "When the Honey Trap left with the kids, he felt like he had nothing farther to live for. Also, he missed the different noises in the house being replaced with total quietness". Most targeted individuals, especially older ones, are more vulnerable because they fear of dying alone. Therefore, they have a greater appreciation for a" Makeshift"family, even though, it is a Honey Trap with a few children. The children give the targeted individual something to look forward and help him forget he is a targeted individual. In many cases, older children will be utilized in the gang stalking scheme and their mother will receive compensation for their participation. On the other hand, sometimes *makeup* families are put together to convey to the targeted individual that they are a unit to get him to fall for the "bait". He may see them in a park near his home, daily. Like we expressed earlier, once you are involved with a Honey Trap it is very difficult to sever the bond. The organizers are constantly utilizing techniques to keep the targeted individual *"unhinged"*.All gang stalkers are not created, many are bought by gifts including a host a family and friends. According to Fictional Wrestler the Million Dollar Man, Ted Dibiase," Everyone can be bought, everybody has a price". Therefore, it would be easier to give a cash strapped family a few dollars to watch and gang stalk an unsuspecting family. The government agencies catalog and watch family members also, this means that they already know their weaknesses. If there is someone who loves women, the organizers who forgo the gift cards and get him a woman instead. Just say a sister has a crack problem, then they will give he money or buy drugs to feed her craving. This includes a wife and the biological children who most likely are in a rocky relationship to take money and gift and target a father in his own home. Many wives are compromised and secretly commune with investigators or agents covertly seek to bring down their own husbands. There have been cases where the wife and his mistress secretly worked together to bring down the "Mark". Many wives and family members who work with investigators are coerced to participate and many do reluctantly. They are willing to work with these illegal programs because they fear they may be targeted or have an opportunity to escape prosecution. The Honey Trap wives may seek to put the targeted individual on child support in which they know he has no means of paying which is a scheme to have him incarcerated. Even when the targeted individual aims to exit the relationship his children are used as a trump card to make him come right back to turmoil. These actions of children are not just identified with Honey Traps, but many women in the world. The Honey Trap is willing to do whatever hurts the targeted individual the most. If the targeted individual becomes hungry, homeless, and alone it would make no difference to the Honey Trap because she is totally detached from the "Mark".

6. Property Attained

The targeted individuals may have no choice but to remain with a Honey Trap because he may not have anywhere to go. Many Honey Traps will scheme to get homes, cars, and bank accounts put in their names to control everything. Most times, the targeted individual is oblivious the woman he is in love with is robbing him blind. She is more willing to engage in these felon type behaviors because she has protection from the government and feels there would be no repercussions. To make the program work efficiently, many are employed to secretly watch the targeted individual. During the honeymoon phase, the Honey Trap property may be jointly attained assets with the targeted individual to give her access to everything he owns. When you have a Honey Trap that resides in your home disgruntled you must to sleep with both eyes open. The Honey Trap is purposefully put in place to cause chaos. They are trained to get your name on as much property as possible; including life insurance policies. Many policies are taken out without your prior knowledge. I recently had a college classmate which I believe succumb to the wrath of a woman which got a large insurance policy on him before taking his life. Under further investigation, this was the second husband which died of mysterious circumstances married to this woman which was charged with both of their murders. If the targeted individual marries the Honey Trap, she has the power to get him committed if he complains about his targeting. In this case, all the property and belongings would fall under the control of the Honey Trap. In case of illness, a Honey Trap wife would have the last say about plans of treatment and the ways in which doctors must proceed. This becomes a sticking point because a lot of assets may lead her to make nefarious decisions on his care and after treatment. Remember, most Honey Traps do not have the targeted individual's best interest in mind. She is financially greedy and is only concerned with her pockets. Back in the '90s, Anna Nicole Smith was accused by a man's family members of being a Honey Trap put in place to cipher the riches of an oil tycoon. The Honey Trap is willing to absolutely take whatever is not **"nailed down"** from the targeted individual including his life. We are certain that there has been an occasion where Honey Traps have attained feelings for her **"Mark"**, but rest assured, she was not able to continue in the line of work for long because they are paid to be heartless. These women have an **"it's them or Me"** kind of perception and money is their driving force. I believe it takes a special kind of female to fill the role of a Honey trap because the average woman cannot be that cold and cunning. This will not necessarily include all Honey Traps because some are forced or coerced into service. These women not only operate with targeted individuals they operate in every aspect of society. These women have discovered their bodies can be used as a sexual weapon.

7. Hope They Can Change Them

Many targeted individuals believe that they can convert a Honey Trap from her gang stalking ways, but in most cases, their efforts are wasteful because shes love the lure of the position in which she is being paid to perform. These women in most cases have a black heart and money is their only motivation and king. It does not matter how good you are to a Honey Trap she will always be a gang stalker. **First,** the Honey Trap does not view you as a companion but more of an objective. **Secondly,** she will not allow herself to get to close to the "mark" meaning you. Many Honey Traps are given the same training as double and secret agents on complex international missions. They are paid not to care, be concerned, and they certainly do not want to be with a targeted individual. These are the type of women who will watch you slowly die, daily, and have no sympathy for you. Most of these women are narcissistic and are devoid of love and compassion which are the reason they are chosen for the mission. As with gang stalkers being handpicked so are these murderous women. To have hope in one of these women could lead to your demise or anyone close to you which tries to interrupt her objectives. Most of these women have the compassion of a maniac and have no cares in the world, but answering to their superiors and getting paid. These women have absolutely no value to the government, are highly expendable, and can easily be replaced. As a matter of fact, if the targeted individual would hurt or murder one of them, then it fits into the depopulation program which is being operated. As with the targeted individuals, Honey Traps are being monitored day and night, but are being brainwashed by their superiors that the targeted individual is the problem. The Honey Traps main weapon is to come with love and affection, ensnare a targeted individual, and lead him to prison, mental institution, or suicide. Many targeted individuals are sitting in prison over a stripper, gang stalker, or prostitute which they had hopes of changing. It is impossible to change someone who does not want to change. Her stringing you along does not mean she has feeling for you, you are being used for conveniences. With Honey Trap/gold-digging women, we must be willing to **"Chalk it up "**to experience and **"Let it be"** because an effort of changing them will fall on **"Deaf ears"**.The odds are heavily against any Honey Trap converting and become a decent person because her only desire is to look for her next **"mark"**. Remember, these women have been psychologically damaged and they are devoid of love and compassion. Most of these women get a thrill seeing others tortured and harmed, narcissistic. According to Mayoclinic.com, "Narcissistic personality disorder — one of several types of personality disorders — is a mental condition in which people have an inflated sense of their own importance, a deep need for excessive attention and admiration, troubled relationships, and a lack of empathy for others. But behind this mask of extreme confidence lies a fragile self-esteem that's vulnerable to the slightest criticism. A narcissistic personality disorder causes problems in many areas of life, such as relationships, work, school or financial affairs. People with narcissistic personality disorder may be generally unhappy and disappointed when they're not given the special favors or admiration they believe they deserve. They may find their relationships unfulfilling, and others may not enjoy being around them.

People with the disorder can:

- Have an exaggerated sense of self-importance
- Have a sense of entitlement and

require constant, excessive admiration

- Expect to be recognized as superior even without achievements that warrant it
- Exaggerate achievements and talents
- Be preoccupied with fantasies about success, power, brilliance, beauty or the perfect mate
- Believe they are superior and can only associate with equally special people
- Monopolize conversations and belittle or look down on people they perceive as inferior
- Expect special favors and unquestioning compliance with their expectations
- Take advantage of others to get what they want
- Have an inability or unwillingness to

recognize the needs and feelings of others

- Be envious of others and believe others envy them
- Behave in an arrogant or haughty manner, coming across as conceited, boastful and pretentious

- Insist on having the best of everything — for instance, the best car or office

At the same time, people with narcissistic personality disorder have trouble handling anything they perceive as criticism, and they can:

- Become impatient or angry when they don't receive special treatment
- Have significant interpersonal problems and easily feel slighted
- React with rage or contempt and try to belittle the other person to make

themselves appear superior

- Have difficulty regulating emotions and behavior
- Experience major problems dealing with stress and adapting to change
- Feel depressed and moody because they fall short of perfection

- Have secret feelings of insecurity, shame, vulnerability and humiliation
  "

Many of these women are indeed beautiful, but the could never truly perceive their value and self-worth as an asset. Honey Traps are highly insecure, immature, and only seeks to satisfy their own desires. Many believe that "things" brings them happiness, but reality has shown, it cannot provide you with decency. Therefore, Sigmund Freud would say these feelings of insecurity and incompleteness would be a woman with a supercharged Id. There are remote cases where these harlots chose to change their nefarious ways. Many love the sport in which they play and for many, it has bought them wealth, recognition and fame. They have an opportunity to rub elbows which many popular individuals. Hopes of changing them, in most cases, are null and void because they are *tailor-made* for the position. They understand and are able to conceive the power in which Delilah had over Samson and are able to use this to the greatest level against the opposition. As stated prior, changing them is *slim to none* especially when they are being paid to perform and are good at their craft. As with Samson, the Philistine Army commanders realized that no matter the physical strength of Samson that sexuality is the one thing he could not resist and their plans were prophetic and effective.

Figure : The Most Strongest Man in the World Could not Resist
The Beauty of Delilah

In the story of Samson and Delilah, Samson was the strongest man in the world but many people don't know that God granted him great wisdom to accompany most of his strength. Despite all the power which the strongest man in the world possessed it was hardly comparable to the human sexual pull of Delilah. The most amazing thing about the story is that Delilah repeatedly requested the secret all his strength and he would provide a riddle to trick her but it would never be the true source of his power which was his hair. Delilah mocked Samson after she tricked him into finding out the source of his strength. According to Judge 16, " he fell in love with a woman in the Valley of Sorek whose name was Delilah. Philistines went to her and said, "See if you can lure him into showing you the secret of his great strength and how we can overpower him so we may tie him up and subdue him. Each one of us will give you eleven hundred shekels of silver."6 So Delilah said to Samson, "Tell me the secret of your great strength and how you can be tied up and subdued."...Samson answered her, "If anyone ties me with seven fresh bowstrings that have not been dried, I'll become as weak as any other man."8 Then the rulers of the Philistines brought her seven fresh bowstrings that had not been dried, and she tied him with them. 9 With men hidden in the room, she called to him, "Samson, the Philistines are upon you!" But he snapped the bowstrings as easily as a piece of string snaps when it comes close to a flame. So the secret of his strength was not discovered....Then she said to him, "How can you say, 'I love you,' when you won't confide in me? This is the third time you have made a fool of me and haven't told me the secret of your great strength." 16 With such nagging she prodded him day after day until he was sick to death of it. 17 he told her everything. "No razor has ever been used on my head," he said, "because I have been a Nazirite dedicated to God from my mother's womb. If my head were shaved, my strength would leave me, and I would become as weak as any other man."18 When Delilah saw that he had told her everything, she sent word to the rulers of the Philistines, "Come back once more; he has told me everything." So the rulers of the Philistines returned with the silver in their hands. 19 After putting him to sleep on her lap, she called for someone to shave off the seven braids of his hair, and so began to subdue him...and his strength left him. 20 Then she called, "Samson, the Philistines are upon you!"He awoke from his sleep and thought, "I'll go out as before and shake myself free." But he did not know that the Lord had left

97

him". In the Story of Samson and Delilah, the Philistine Army was unable to stop Samson because of his incredible strength and power. As with other rulers of the world, they employed the services of a Honey Trap, Delilah, and he knew she wanted to know the contents of his strength but she had Samson in a state in which he was "silly putty" in her hands. The Philistine Rulers understood Samson's incredible power and his only weakness, his emotions. Samson was aware Delilah was a Philistine and she tried to trick him several times, but armed with this information, he still took a chance. As with Samson, most "Marks" have reasons to believe that they are being "Duped" but continue with the fling or relationship. Even in politics, many believed Monica Lewinsky was a paid Honey Trap put in place to take down the most powerful man in the world at that time, President Bill Clinton. Therefore, many in organized community gang stalking employ the services of beautiful maidens to come in and allow them to access the nearly impossible places and operate as powerful as the most trained professional agent.

8.Feeling Hopelessness, Despaired, Lonely Not Being Able To Find Another Companion

The feeling of hopelessness and depression is one of the greatest hallmarks of these illegal covert community gang stalking programs. The Honey Trap is intended to get close to the targeted individual and break his confidence completely down. The Honey Trap is constantly pipelined instructions from her superiors to ensure that every move she makes is full of grace and professional. The government seeks imperfections in the early stages of the gang stalking scheme which the Honey Trap can come and fully exploit to farther attack in the later parts of the program. The goal of the program is to leave the targeted individual in a psychotic frame of mind and totally void of reality. The Honey Trap is also put in place to guarantee that the targeted individual does not find anyone who will be beneficial to his well being. Each female who makes acquaintance with the targeted individual has a threat level assigned and the emphasis is put upon that person until the threat is resolved. Honey Traps are particularly aware of individuals which may have the unfortunate luck of being gang stalked themselves and she wants to make sure they do not create a bond or an alliance. The Honey Trap will team up with family members which are accusing the targeted individual of suffering from a mental situation and she will propel their ideologies by her first-hand observations and accounts. She moves carefully that all her actions are covert and hidden from the targeted individual. She openly reminds the targeted individual that she is the best woman he could ever get and no one would want to be with someone experiencing the difficulties which he has in his life. She also reminds him that his actions have totally destroyed their relationship and asks," **Why can't it be the way it used to be**".When most targeted individuals eventually wake up their lives are in total disrepair to the point where they have lost all their remaining friends, family, and are in total isolation after the Honey Trap abandons them. Good Honey Traps ensure that the targeted individual is 100% broken and he will need years of counseling just to become the person when they first met. She will do subtle things to remind the targeted individual whom he was before the gang stalking took over his life. She may conveniently leave an old snapshot of a Christmas party when the targeted individual was having the time of his life. The Honey Trap needs to *jackhammer* the fact home that the reason the targeted individual lost everything is his own fault with no one to blame for his misfortune. She will remind him of all the great things going on in the lives of her friends to plow the fact home that the targeted individual is living in a state of misery and things will never get better. Small things like public embarrassments will be used by the Honey Trap to *key in* on the targeted individual's level of worthlessness. The power of the tongue is a powerful and deadly weapon when it is used in the correct way. The food channel star Anthony Bourdain was one of the most popular shows on prime time; and, at the height of his success, he committed suicide. Many were amazed because he had a dream job where he would travel around the world tasting different foods and experiencing different cultures. Most did not know Anthony had a girlfriend half of his age which would ridicule him on the regular; and only a few hours before his untimely death she told him, "Kill your self I don't care". It is widely believed that he committed suicide to garner her affection. Even in death, she posted her last text message to him on her social media account. It is amazing the way the power of perception could have on a person's life. This is the goal of this government this private covert program to totally destroy the target individual and many who are associated with him. Mr. Bourdain had just completed an episode of his wildly popular show, Part Unknown, in the swamps of Louisiana and he did not show signs of distress. Generally, this man was the life of the party without a care in the world. This lady was virtually unknown and she was believed to be able to breakdown one of the most beloved men in recent times. Honey Traps which work in the capacity of mistresses may blackmail the targeted individual at one period of their engagement. The targeted individual in a suppressed state is often too vulnerable to leave the hostile relationship because the fear of being totally alone and might fear there would be a loss of sexual companionship. Being alone is the driving for which causes many individuals to commit suicide or stop caring about life although. The psychologist which helped to organized these gang stalking programs are fully aware of this type of gravitation pull being alone has on the psyche of many individuals; especially those which have been targeted. Notwithstanding years of opposition, a Honey Trap comes along and adds insult and injury to his already troubled life.

CHAPTER 7

THE KINDS OF HONEY TRAPS

The Several Kinds Of Honey Traps

A. Short-Term Honey Trap:

This particular Honey Trap is used for one-night affairs and is usually sexy, seductive, and someone who is able to stand out in a crowded room. These Honey Traps are most times prostitutes, call girls, strippers, and ladies of the evening. Their job is to entice the targeted individual with pure sexuality and nothing promised beyond that point. These Honey Traps are trained more intensely; than other Honey Traps, because she has to get the targeted individual to trust her in a shorter period of time. Sexual intercourse must provide to be her most convincing asset which will leave the targeted individual in a deep resting state. These women are trained to move quickly and provide their service with thrust, intensity, and they must convince him of their bodily. They cannot come on too strong because it would be a red flag to the targeted individual. They must stay away from words such as love, future, and children and use vocals during sexual orientation. Sometimes these kinds of Honey Traps work in brothel or sex groups to team up on one "Mark".

There Are Several Features Which The Short Term Honey Trap provides.

1. Their tenure can last from a few hours to several weeks.

2. The engagement must be high sexual energy and intensity.

3. They must convince the targeted individual they are harmless and complete their task in a relatively

   short period of time

4. They must establish a clear vantage point

of the area and make a mental note of where everything is located. For example, they need to see where the targeted individual puts his wallet and keys. Furthermore, they need to establish all exits of the dwelling to ensure they can make a hasty retreat in case their cover is blown.

5. Many cases, they want to be soothing to the Targeted Individual in cases, where he may just need someone to just talk to.

6. If they meet in a bar/club they must get the targeted individual as drunk

as possible by keeping a bunch of drinks flowing because this will impair his judgment. Many of these women are model material with great bodies and must make the targeted individual feel he is **"lucky"**, **"Hit the Jackpot"**, and she will give him a **"night to remember"**. Therefore, she is given the task of convincing the targeted individual she would give him everything he wants. Some women come from prostitution stings and they have already been educated by street pimps and they are encouraged to utilize all the tricks of the trade. Honey Traps are taught early to leave the Targeted individual financially broke without recourse.

Duties Of A Short Term Honey Trap

1. Sexual Satisfaction. The goal of the Short Term Honey Trap is to absolutely blow the Targeted Individual's mind with sex, drug, alcohol and other mischievous activities.

2. Study the perimeter, especially a home or workplace, and mentally catalog all parts of the location.

3. Plant evidence of a crime or convince the targeted individual to engage in illegal behavior which will

be used against him later. For example, former Washington Mayor, Marion Barry, alludes that he was set up by several

Honey Traps, including a girlfriend, in an FBI *sting smoking crack in a hotel room..*

4. Take vital information from the targeted individual's home, car, or place of employment and give it to the Handlers. These women are taught to rob and take anything of value. For example: rolex, check book, wallet

5. Locate, destroy, and retrieve evidence at the discretion of the leaders of the program which will

incriminate the Targeted Individual

6. Lead the Targeted Individual to a destination in which he would not go on his own. Example: Drug House, Meth Lab, or a seedy part of town. She may arrange drug buy and have him busted as soon as he leaves the residence.

7. Video tape or record any sexual activity to ensure she gains leverage over the Targeted Individual in the short period she

works with him. This type of Honey Traps seeks to exploit or extort the Targeted Individual after a one time sexual encounter. Ensure she get the Targeted Individual to talk

as much as possible.

8. Drug the Targeted Individual or get him high to guarantee she attains the necessary information for Handlers.

9. If she has kids then she will use them to get the Targeted Individual to let his guards down.

10. Of all the other Honey Traps, she is the one which will almost certainly get the Targeted Individual set up in a shady fashion. Honey Traps are not limited to only the Targeted Individual Program because they have been highly utilized in political circles to find damming evidence of someone holding a high position. For example, many critics believe that President

Trump was light upon the Russian tampering probe because they had information which could have hurt his presidency. Democrats delved deeply into the probes to discover the reasons in which President Trump was so lenient in such a critical assessment. As a matter of fact, many politicians and public figures have been caught in an array of sexual indiscretions that have harmed their political careers. Most times, these Honey Traps bring drugs to the room or location to ensure that the targeted individual will become entrapped. The Honey Trap ploy has been used in many countries, for years, and a countless number of people have lost everything because of these seductive women of mystic mindset.

B. Mid-Term Honey Trap:

The midterm Honey Trap has nearly the same duties as the regular Honey Trap, but they must complete their tasks in a shorter period of time. Many Midterm Honey Traps may become a long term Honey Trap if their assignment is not completed within a timely fashion or she is dealing with a particularly difficult targeted individual. The midterm Honey Trap must embody a high level of sexuality, as with the short term Honey Trap, and combine the passion utilized by the Long term Honey Trap. Most of her language will be the same as the long term Honey Trap, but just complete her within a shorter period of time.

Characteristics of Mid Term Honey Trap.

1. Sex and seduction are used as a weapon to have targeted individuals obey.

2. She will toy with his emotions and talk about future plans.

3. She will leave him with nearly no notice and make him believe

   he did something wrong.

4. She will patiently wait to identify weakness and then seek to set him up.

5. She may act like she is fleeing an abusive relationship to "thumb along" the Targeted Individual.

6. Unlike the short and long term Honey Traps, the midterm Honey Trap may be asked to reprise several small roles such as leaving and coming back to keep the target individual life in a "tailspin".

7. The Mid Term Honey Trap is engaged from several weeks to multiple months.

8. Many Mid Term Honey Traps are similar to a side women or sexual fling which lasts a few weeks.

9. Mid Term Honey Traps, Through sexual influence, will try to get the Targeted Individual to sign over important property.

10. Mid Term Honey Trap, like her other counterparts, have not feelings for her intended victim. Many of the midterm Honey Traps may serve as girlfriend, lover, and confidant. Her job is to give the target individual a burst of satisfaction for a reasonable period of time. She will be cautious not to have children or make too many promises she will not be able to carry forth. As with all Honey Traps, she will be put in place to gaslight the targeted individual that his gang stalking does not exist. She is the first person to say, " Your suffering from anxiety".

C. Long Term Honey Traps:

The Long Term Honey Trap is similar to a secret agent with a deep cover for many years. Most often, these particular women are reserved for high-value targets which must be *chipped away for* years. Most high-value targets have little trust for anyone, but like all men, he has desires to commingle with the opposite sex. An efficient Honey Trap can get close to him, even if he as a good wife at home, and can maneuver more stealth that a seasoned agent. She could open doors in which no one has ever enter and gain a considerable amount of trust in a duration of time. With a high-level target individual, sex is insufficient to capture their attention. Everything must be loyalty over a proven period to time. This also is true with high dignitaries of the world, they are totally immune to the average Honey Trap and can smell their roost a mile away. The perception of a long term Honey Trap characteristics must be identified by their patience and willingness to earn his trust over an extended level of time. Long term Honey Traps can be wives, mistresses, or even confidants, but their effectiveness will be based on their level of skill. In most cases, Honey Traps are close in proximity to the targeted individual and share multiple similarities. In many cases, they may be the educated homemaker type which must be employed for the task to get close to this important gentleman.

Characteristics Of a Long Term Honey Trap

1. Long Term Honey Traps are willing to be patient and wait to capture the necessary information from the Targeted Individual despite the duration of time.

2. From the first meeting, she is constantly talking about developing a family structure to create an advantage over the Targeted Individual.

3. Nearly all Long Term Honey Traps and the Targeted Individual resides in the same home one point or another.

4. A great number of Long Term Honey Traps exchanged vows with the Targeted Individual to break him down emotionally.

5. Long Term Honey Traps are generally reserved to top level Targeted Individuals which are difficult to capture or "crack".

6. Long Term Honey Traps have access to capital, billing statements, wills, dossiers, properties, and all vital statistics of the Targeted Individual.

7. Long Term Honey Traps may choose to have a child(ren) for the targeted individual to soft his stance and become more conducive to the investigation or plot.

8. Long Term Honey Traps usually attain better pay, than her Honey Traps counterparts , because the access of information which is available to her over a period of time.

9. Long Term Honey Traps are highly cultured and educated because of the high power gentlemen which they are assigned.

10. Despite the span of time residing with the Targeted Individual she will acquire

absolutely no feelings. In many case she will be with him until death.

D. Honey Dick

Many are unaware that there is a male counterpart to the Honey Trap and he is called the **Honey Dick.** This man is paid to assume the same role as the female Honey Trap but from a male perspective. This person would come in and ruin the targeted female credit, finance, sleep with her friends, steal her property, and abandon her as quickly as he came. His job is to come in and destroy the little life she has after gang stalking. Most Honey Dicks are in their twenties, but some can range from any age according to the desires of the female "Mark".

Figure : College Graduate Student

One requirement is this man is unusually
well endowed, genital wise than the
average man to help convince the female-
targeted individual that he will be the best

she has ever had. Many Honey Dicks serves dual purposes because they target both women and men which may have homosexual desires. Despite the assignment, the Honey Dick's job is to set you up, leave you broke, homeless, and depressed. Generally, Honey Dicks and Honey Traps work many cases in a calendar year and have no allegiance to anyone but financial gain. It has been reported by numerous female-targeted individuals that these Honey Dicks will secretly put their victims on the dark website via the human sex trafficking ring where individuals will pay to see their intimate moments with the Honey Dick. Amazingly his intentions are kept silent and an unsuspecting female-targeted individual may be broadcast, nightly, via the world wide web. This is a traumatic effect because she has to relive much of the frustration, over and over. Another female-targeted individual got in a serious relationship with a Honey Dick and did not realize this man was already married with an entire family two states over. His wife was well aware of his employment, as a Honey Dick, and had no problems with his position. As a matter of fact, they would make games that she was taking care of his entire family. The sad part about these types of stories is that they are able to get away with such evil behavior and able to hurt good people which only are pursuing genuine affection. It must be noted that when these types of images are circulated on the dark web it impossible to detain. The closest example would be like taking a pillow, stuffed with small feathers, and opening a window on the top floor of a building and releasing them on a windy day. It would be impossible to find each feather because they have traveled many distances.

Figure: Part Time Computer Analylist

Nearly all those which deal with Honey

Traps or Honey Dicks are fully aware they are getting played, but they just can't resist someone showering them with attention. Many high community officials have fallen prey to either the Honey Trap or Honey Dick because of the allure and attractiveness of these beautiful individuals. Many Honey Dicks come from the porn industry, exotic male Dancers, and foreign destinations to grab the attention of the Female Targeted Individual.

Characteristics Of A Honey Dick

1. His main job is to "screw" the female Targeted Individual into submission as much as possible to break her down.

2. Desires to meet all the female Targeted Individual friends.

3. Earn her trust in a short period of time by telling her she is special and he has never met anyone like her before.

4.When dealing with older, female Targeted

Individual he will constantly remind her she looks good for her age.

5.   After a short period of time, he will complaint about he has a financial obligation in which he does not know where to come up with the funds. He knows she will volunteer.

6.   Will be elusive and hard to "nail down" about his past and seek to get early commitments from the female Targeted Individual.

7.   He will seek to avoid members of her family and friends which may not approved the relationship.

8.   Similar to the Honey Traps, he will not attain absolutely no feeling for the female Targeted Individual believe she is getting what she deserves.

9.   The Honey Dick will do **anything his Handlers   request   including   poisoning, robbing, or setting up the Female Targeted**

Individual

10. He will immediately take control of her house and car without recourse and take whatever he chooses. Many will try to video tape any sexual interactions to be sold or circulated for profits.

How To Identify a Honey Trap

The reason that Honey Traps are so difficult to identify is that they are able to blend in with most of society and they approach you at times when you are vulnerable. These Honey Traps come in saying all the right things at the right time. Most will befriend the targeted individual to mask their devious assignment. For example, a lovely cashier which you see at the corner store whenever you make groceries and you greet each other with a pleasant smile and warm conversations. You can tell she likes you by your level of eye contact, smiles, and interactions. You exchange numbers and begin to casually see each other and go out on a few dates. Little do you know that this woman was strategically placed in your pathway by getting *an agreed* job at the corner supermarket you frequent. She is given your profile and studies your likes and dislikes. Generally, this woman knows everything about you. This is the kind of person that can be used as a deep-cover Honey Trap. Also, the Honey Trap business is a lucrative operation because many Honey Dicks sell their sexual exploits with the female-targeted individual on the web, as mentioned earlier. Several female-targeted individuals have horrified stories where their private moments had been sold for profit by the person they love and trust. Nearly all female-targeted individuals who become involved with Honey Dicks will most likely end up heartbroken, confused, and alone. Despite the hardship and pain, many strong, male and female, targeted individuals have the strength to bounce back. After a period of time, the Honey Trap or Honey Dick becomes equal to a drug user is well informed the drug is helping to destroy their lives, but the sweet fragrant and the high the drug user receives makes it impossible for them to get off of **"Cloud 9"**. The sexual basis of the relationship makes it nearly impossible to say "No" and the more they attempt to say "No" their body and actions will say "Yes"; this is the epitome of temptation at its finest. The Honey Trap's goal is to take control of your body, mind, soul, and possess the fiber of your being. Of course, we are mostly referring to the Long term Honey Traps, but its relatively the same as short term Honey Traps, the actions are completed in a shorter period of time. They are specially trained to complete their plots in a short time span usually because of information needed more relatively. There is absolutely no difference in terms of goals or outcomes, the targeted individual is left broken. All Honey Traps**(Or Honey Tramps in its street terms)** or designated to destroy the lives of those in which they come in contact.

How Do Honey Traps Get Paid

Honey Traps are paid handsomely, based on the task involved, and the greater the assignment the more the compensation. It has been reported some Honey Traps have been given mansions, expensive cars, trips to the most exotic destinations, and huge sums of money.

Figure: Lovely Honey Trap Expensive Vacation

According to the assignment, some frequent the ritziest clubs, exclusive facilities, and rub elbows with the elites of society. This is not the case with those who are assigned to the targeted individual. Those which are assigned to a targeted individual usually receive less because most are stripped of their finances. In many cases, the length of time has no bearing because and short term Honey Traps could attain information quicker than a long term Honey Trap. In terms of greater assets and property attainment, the long term Honey Trap would be greater for the task and would be compensated more revenue because of her dedication to the project. Some Honey Traps only get reimbursed small trinkets while others are awarded free college educations, homes, cars, and large bonuses. In many cases, the revenue and other financial assets achieved during the scheme of deceiving targeted individuals many Honey Trap may be permitted to keep. For example, a car that has been placed in the name of both the Honey Trap and the targeted individual; and, this extends to child support, homes, property, and promotions. This is the reason it is so difficult to get a Honey Trap to change her *"colors"*. This makes someone with a limited education feel important to be working with law enforcement; especially if she comes from the opposite side of the tracks. In short, the importance of getting paid outweighs decency, sympathy, empathy, and all forms of compassion. The purse is where their heart is and they are living for the moment, right now. The new Honey Traps are willing to go to church to gang stalk because neither God nor faith will keep them from being paid. For finances, these women are willing to lose their soul and they have already made a deal with the devil, unknowingly. That is correct, the Honey Trap program has a spiritual aspect because you are exchanging your soul for gifts and riches. Therefore, Honey Traps can be paid with job advancements, favors in court cases, avoidance of prison time for them and relatives, and special treatment in a difficult situation. The spiritual component takes place because it is a form of human sacrifice in which they are participating and their souls are put up for grabs. Many of these women operate through standard gang stalking apps which has all the targeted individuals' information uploaded. In rare cases, if they are out, she might be asked to gang stalk another targeted individual in the vicinity. Their job is to follow the targeted individual, step for step. Some Honey Traps have received free college tuition or student loans forgiveness for assisting with the organized community gang stalking program. Mostly strippers, prostitutes, call girls, college students, and sometimes runaways are used as "human bait" to entrap and targeted individuals. The majority are beautiful women with appeasing bodies that are sweet on the eyes. Huge breasts, smooth skin, thick thighs, and great big butts are the attributes that attract men to them.

Figure: French Maiden Honey Trap From Paris, France

During the investigative stage, they catalog whether the targeted individual is attracted to certain body parts like breast, butts, or size and with a *fast-food* precision the governmental program is able to serve up the exact woman in which they desire. In 2015, Dr. Uma Johnson believed that he was the victim of a Honey Trap that came in and embraced his ideologies and even dressed the exact ways he believed that women should dress; including hair and skin preparation. It was later discovered that Dr. Johnson was intimate with this female and he later found out this woman was a known stripper. Engaging stripper which goes against his beliefs of black righteousness and many questioned choices after that point.

7. Ways To Identify A Honey Trap

1. People Which Meet You and Have Everything in Common.

This is the calling card of the Honey Trap scheme is that, within the first few days to a week, you eerily have everything in common. They hone in on all your likes and dislikes. From a Targeted Individual's standpoint that would be mimicking it is a bit harder to identify because it is the opposite sex. They are designed to mirror all of your likes and dislikes. This would be one of the greatest red flags to let you know this person may be a government agent. There is no way that absolutely no two people would have everything exactly like this would be beyond ridiculous. This does not mean that the person is not genuine, but it denotes that you must move with extreme caution. For example: if you take a shot of wine from Brazil and you get a quick buzz, then this means that you must be careful from that point because to consume too much would lead to a hangover. In this tell sign, it means to do an assessment of the female's likes and dislikes, which are not yours and wait for her answers. It's similar to throwing a monkey wrench in a meat grinder to see if it could process it. For example, I hate dew melons make my skin crawl and wait for her answer. She has been programmed that you love dew melons, either she won't reply or will be confused about how to answer. She thinks for a moment then sheepishly responds, "I don't like them either" You reply, "I gotcha, I love dew melons", and wait, then She jokingly says, " I was just kidding, love them too". If this is the case, then it is a good chance this person has been studying your profile and mimicking your likes and dislikes. Run multiple mini-assessments to determine whether she is truthful or a phony agent placed to destroy your life.

2. **They will Act Like You Are the Greatest Lover in the World.**

This scheme may be more difficult to identify, but it still not impossible. Whenever she repeats how great you are sexually, completely ignore her and provide zero feedback. She needs to know you are "biting" and the direction she needs to continue to get you completely "hooked". Therefore, it is imperative that you never tell them how great they are, in the first days to a week, simply act like it is just a good time. This will confuse the Honey Trap and she will not know the way in which she should proceed. IF YOU THAT GREAT IN THE SACK, her responses should not change because you are doing exactly the same things.

3. **Someone "Wines and Dines" You in a Short Period of Time**

This is one of the plots which run where a person you meet, in a relatively short period of time, spends tons of money on you and provides expensive gifts.

Figure: Expensive Cars, Vacations, and Ritzy Restaurants

In this scheme, they most likely, are having to exchange the sex factor for expensive items and good treatment, but this plot is equally as deadly. Despite the method used, you still have become a slave under their influence or love spell. The head of these illegal covert government programs doesn't mind spending eight hundred dollars to wine, dine, and entwine you. They may feel this is a small expense taking into account the thousands their Honey Trap will get off of you and the worth of the information gathered. The way in which you can curve their aggression with this tactic is to write down every single item they spend upon you and promise it will be paid back. This sends a message that you understand nothing is free, in this world, and you fully are willing to give them back their stuff if the time span allots. You need to send them a message that their gifts, sex, and seduction is not enough to reel you in and they must prove their sincerity. As a matter of fact, these principles can be applied to all relationships. The wine and dine plot is generally used by men, but many times malice could be misinterpreted for someone who is really sincere, therefore do not run good people away being paranoid. As a targeted individual, you must take precautions because this comes with the territory. These types of techniques can be applied to all relationships. The key to dealing with relationships while being a targeted individual is approaching all situations with extreme prejudice and allow things to play themselves out.

4. Someone Whom You Just Requests A Key to Your Home, Accounts Ect....

With this scheme, they have positioned you to give them information which would be vital to your existence and they could use this for extortion purposes. Also, be careful taking risque pictures and videos because later this could be used for leverage. It is not customary for a person who you just meet to ask you for important information and this is a red flag component. To request a key to your home; after only a few days of seeing each other, raises many concerns because your home is your most sacred place of privacy. Time is the thing that must be assessed to determine their level of genuinely and honesty. A host of people have provided strangers with information which was used against them in a malice way. The main function of Honey Traps is to cipher information and provide this to their handlers. Important Dossiers /documents and information may later be used against you, in a court of law. These types of situations occur more often than most would imagine and this is one of the roles of the Honey Trap. Men who fall for the lust and passion of a Honey Trap allows her to take full advantage of them. As a matter of fact, these are the kind of men who are "ripe" for the picking of a Honey Trap. Honey Traps are looking for weak and vulnerable minded men she could have way with.

5. Honey Traps Disguised as Target Individuals.

The weave her web around the intended

tensions of a Honey Trap planted in the community will make all efforts to be in the spaces you attend the most. This is not limited to rallies, media outlets, like Facebook and YouTube, and the community in which the targeted individual resides. It is common knowledge that one of the greatest tricks government officials operate these covert stalking plans is to plant and so-called female-targeted individuals in your city. They understand that most targeted individuals have limited friends, family, and viable contact and they use this to their benefit. By putting a sexy Honey Trap, posing as a targeted individual, in the same city, there is a great chance that you will eventually meet each other. First, the skim allows you to see her on media and she might comment on a post on yours. Second, you see her in the city and lightly recognize who she is and that when the contact has been made. Third, she will be bold with her dislike of the targeted program to convince you she is authentic. This woman will have woven deeply into the targeted community, your community, and it would be difficult to reveal that this female is a deep cover operative. Even for the most seasoned targeted individuals, this may be the one trap they will not be able to evade. Targeted Individual, Decorated Ex Military, Kenneth Peartree, had a Honey Trap, deep cover, planted in his life and the allure was so strong that he did not realize she was an operative until they got divorced. This means despite his level of understanding about the targeted program, it still did not keep him from falling prey to a Honey Trap. Therefore, all targeted individuals must understand when they pull out the Honey Traps they have pulled out the "Big Guns" and it is almost unfair of those being targeted with these types of measures. Whenever encountering a female-targeted individual, you must run a mental, physical, and life background on her to ensure she is truly a targeted individual and not a perp/operative agent. This will be discussed more in-depth in Honey Traps This must be noted that there are many female and male perps in the targeted community. Female targeted individuals who seem too good to be true is also a telling sign that she is a perpetrator. Also, female-targeted individuals who claim they are a targeted individual but do not take the same precautions in protecting themselves as true targeted individuals is a fake.

6. **Honey Traps With Background Cannot Be Validated.**

This is a hot button issue because most Honey Traps create a fake persona and identity just to make your acquaintance.

Therefore, if you are a conscience individual then she must be able to "fit" into the consciousness movement. She will be given a listing of all your influences and will make them hers to have the same things in common. She will want to go to the same rallies and shows you attend. As with the examples above, you must ask for her life background check. This is the kind you attain through life experiences. This means she should be able to backup everything to be validated as a bona fide woman and not a perp. As with all examples, time is the key and preparation to further understand this person's ideology. As in the targeted community, there is an array of perpetrators/ government agents which is the reason you must get to know each female you are involved in. If she is someone you have been dating and things are heating up, then you must at least meet three members of her family or two friends. Honey Traps on assignment rarely speaks of her background because she does not have one outside your profile. The *let downstage* is when she ups and leaves without a trace. Many times, she is instructed to make it look like something you did to let you bear the guilt of ruining a good relationship and this is a key factor in the organized stalking protocol. They need to leave you broken and confused. They have gone as far as perpetrating like the Honey Trap has won the lottery and ran off with another man just to break your heart. Note: it is highly important that they are provided an exiting skit to leave you with the burden of guilt because it is written in their policies. The pull of the Honey Trap on your heart is so strong that you would never be willing to meet another female. Many times, she will tell you she loves you with tongue in cheek because it alone is another lie. Factually, they get amusement from stringing you along and good sex is another bonus from the project.

7. They Constantly Lie or Stretch The Truth

The most evident way to capture a Honey Trap in action is to get catch them in a lie. Most times, Honey Traps have to lie to cover up uncertain truths which means they are unsure about the specifics of how the question refers to the targeted individual. This means that she must *free flow* the answer. Honey Traps are taught to tell you what you want to hear and most of their actions are sexual in nature. The difference between a Honey Trap and uncover agent is that the agent is not permitted to have sexual contact with the "mark", but a Honey Trap, the *sky is the limit* because their work is a covert operation. They lie when they tell you they love you or you are the best person they have been intimate with. They lie when they point out others whom they believe are not good for you and she is doing her best to advance your life. Remember she must keep you intoxicated with sexual satisfaction for the ploy to be effective. You must have a willingness to let your guard completely down and start to trust this woman whom you have met in only a few weeks. She lies when she says the things you share in common. Worldwide term sex-espionage refers to the art of being a Honey Trap and denotes their devilish attributes of breaking down "Marks/Targets" which are deemed impenetrable. *According to Wikipedia, "Sexepionage is the involvement of sexual activity, or the possibility of sexual activity, intimacy, romance, or seduction to conduct espionage. Sex or the possibility of sex can function as a distraction, incentive, cover story, or unintended part of any intelligence operation. Sexepionage is a historically documented phenomenon and even the CIA has previously added Nigel West's work Historical Dictionary of Sexespionage to its proposed intelligence officer's bookshelf. A commonly known type of sexepionage is a Honeytrap operation, which is designed to compromise an opponent sexually".*

CONCLUSION

The usage of Honey Traps has been a viable tool, for many years, to gather difficult information which would otherwise be impossible. Honey Traps have been used since the beginning of time and they play an important part of the illegal targeted individual program. Honey Traps are beautiful, tempting, and seductive and have lead to the ruin of countless human beings. Honey Traps usage has exploded, over the last few years, and there seems to be no stopping with the invent of the illegal governmental watch list. Targeted individuals must be armed with the truth and peep out these illegal and covert operations. Not knowing the past, you will not be able to control your future.